A Walk in the
Park

Written by Sally Hewitt

Photography by Chris Fairclough

W

FRANKLIN WATTS

LONDON•SYDNEY

First published in 2005 by
Franklin Watts
96 Leonard Street
London EC2A 4XD

Franklin Watts Australia
45-51 Huntley Street
Alexandria NSW 2015

© Franklin Watts 2005

Editors: Caryn Jenner, Sarah Ridley
Designer: Louise Best
Art director: Jonathan Hair
Photography: Chris Fairclough
Map: Hardlines

Many thanks to Sylvia, Theo, Rosie, Sasha,
Danny, Liam and Milly for agreeing to appear
in this book.

A CIP catalogue record for this book is
available from the British Library

ISBN 0 7496 6038 4

Dewey decimal classification number: 790.068

Printed in China

Contents

Wide open space

The park is a wide open space
in the middle of the town.
Can you see buildings beyond the trees?

There are so many things to do in the park, you can stay all day.

Games on the grass

The grass is a good place to run as fast as you can!

Some children are learning
to play football.
What other games could
you play on the grass?

Boating lake

Children learn to sail on the boating lake. You are not allowed to swim in the water!

Water birds swim on the lake. They come to the edge looking for food.

The playground

In the playground you can climb the scramble net.

If you are thirsty, you can drink at the water fountain.

The water is shallow in the paddling pool.

Swings and slides

There are swings, slides and climbing frames in the playground. Why is the floor soft and springy?

A fence round the playground
keeps children in and dogs out.

Bowling and putting

Adults bowl on the smooth grass of the bowling green.

Children play mini-golf on the putting green.

Which game would you like to play?

The scent of flowers is all around as you walk under the pergola.

The café

An ice-cream from the café cools you down on a hot day. What would you buy on a cold day?

All the flowers in the flower bed
by the café are red or pink.

Tennis courts

A tall fence keeps the balls in the tennis court area. Why do you think the fence is made of wire?

The courts look like grass, but they are made of astroturf.

Looking after the park

The park is big. It's hard
work looking after it.
What could you do to help
look after the park?

Why do park staff use tractors?

Park bench

There are benches to sit on
all around the park.
It is good to have a rest.

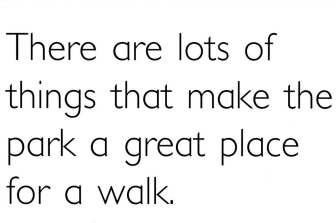

There are lots of
things that make the
park a great place
for a walk.

Map

You can start a walk from any point on a map. To follow the walk in this book, put your finger on **Start** and trace the route.

Key

open space

boating lake

playground

bowling green

putting green

flowers

tennis court

bench

tractor

car park

litter bin

pergola

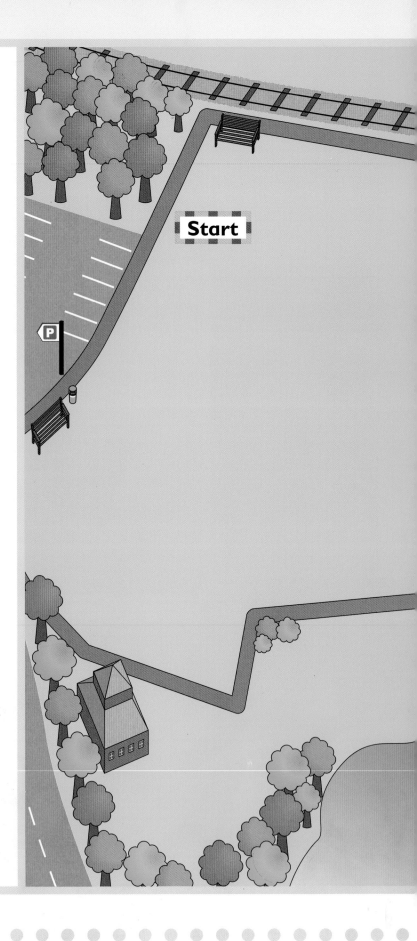

Start

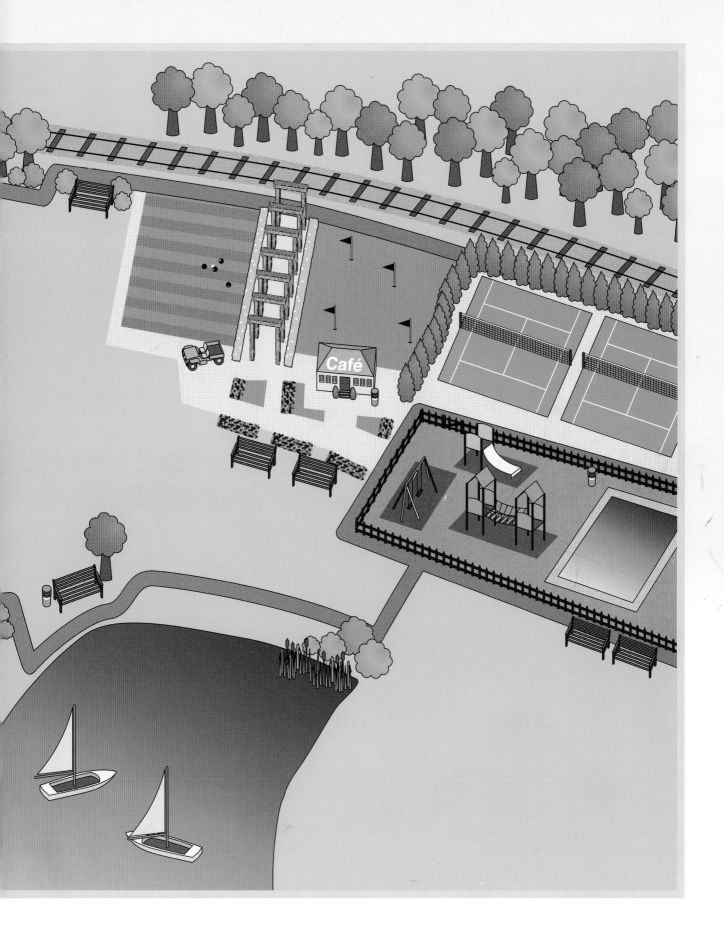

Quiz

A park is a green space in a busy town.
What surrounds a town park?

Look at page 6.

Boats sail on the boating lake. What else might you see on the lake?

Look at pages 10 and 11.

Children play in the playground.
What helps to keep them safe?

Look at pages 12 to 15.

There is grass, water and
astroturf in the park.
What sports can you
play in the park?

Look all through the book.

There are plenty of jobs to
be done in the park.
Who works in the park?

Look at page 23.

All kinds of plants grow in
the park.
Can you name some
of them?

Look all through the book.

Index